Optimal Levels!

FUN FLAVOR
BOOK 2

ROBERT S. MURPHY

Deeper
Understanding
Books

All graphics and layouts by Robert S. Murphy
Optimal Levels! is based on CREAME pedagogy
(Consciousness Raising, Emotions Analysis, Manipulation, and Expression)

CREAME and *Optimal Levels!* designed by Robert S. Murphy

Copyright © 2010 by Robert S. Murphy
Deeper Understanding Books
1-6-12 Ongagawa, Onga-cho
Onga-gun. Fukuoka, Japan 811-4307

www.murphyschool.com

All rights reserved. No part of the material protected by this copy right notice may be reproduced or utilized in any form by any means, electronic or mechanical, including photocopying, recording, or by any information storage and retrieval system, without written permission from the copyright holder.

Printed in the United States of America

About this series

Welcome to the **OPTIMAL LEVELS!** series. This series is probably unlike any series of textbooks that you have encountered in the past. These textbooks have been designed to maximize student thinking and foster the construction of cognitive skills through the usage of the English language. This series is based upon my own research in *Mind, Brain, and Education* at Harvard University and my Master's research in TEFL/TESL at the University of Birmingham.

You will find no rote memorization tasks here -and there are no grammar boxes either! *"Deeper Understanding"* is really about the ability to solve puzzles and problems in the real world. Memorization tasks and grammar boxes have little impact on dynamically changing real world issues. Rather than *presenting* to students what must be learned, this series proposes motivating themes and scaffolded tasks that are designed to build skills <u>dynamically</u>. By doing the theme-based student-centered tasks, students dynamically learn and understand language usage by creating the skills necessary to negotiate meaning and build upon what they already know.

This series is about building *real skills* that will work in the *real world*. It is based on cutting-edge research in neuroscience and psychology. Enjoy exploring the creation of these dynamic skills that will lead to the *deeper understanding* of English and beyond!

Robert S. Murphy, series author
Deeper Understanding Books

Optimal Levels! Fun Flavor Book 2

Modules	Themes	Optional
Module 1	Sports	The Suitcase
Module 2	Music	Happy Shopping
Module 3	Fashion	Moving Pictures
Module 4	Night Life	The Chef
Module 5	Eating Out	Handheld Games
Module 6	Parks	The Convertible

How to use this book (it's all about building skills!)

Teachers, adjust the following instructions to match your students' levels.

Section 1. Introduction

Look carefully at the provided picture. This picture represents the theme for this entire unit. What questions can you come up with? Think and then write down three more *"who, what, when, where, why, and how"* questions. After you have written the questions in the boxes, think of answers to your own questions and write them down too. Find a partner. Ask your questions to your partner and then write your partner's answers in the boxes next to your own answers. *How different were your answers?*

Feelings/emotions from the picture: Write down one or two feelings/emotions that you get from the picture.

Performance of Understanding Time! Find a partner. Discuss how the picture makes you feel and why. Compare answers with your partner. *How different were your answers?* Discuss with your teacher!

Section 2. Word map to expression!

Choose one word (or one phrase) as the *Root Word* for the word map. The Root Word can be anything that you think matches this module's theme. Write the Root Word in the middle of the word map. Use your imagination and connect as many first generation links to other words as possible. Decide if the connections are positive or negative. Write a *plus (+)* or a *minus (-)* mark in the small circles. Next, use your imagination and create second generation connections. Write a *plus (+)* or a *minus (-)* mark in the small circles. There are eight 'floating connections'. Use these as you wish. You can make them first, second, or even third generation connections.

Find three Main Ideas... Look carefully at your completed word map. *Do you see any patterns? Do you see some common ideas?* Think carefully and write down three Main Ideas that strongly connect to the Root Word.

Self-assessment of sentences: Think about your work in Section 2. *Did you do well?* Give yourself a score! [Scoring: 1 is low and 5 is high.]

Section 3. Expansion

Write your three Main Ideas in the white boxes. Find at least two linguistic, socio-cultural, and feelings/emotional connections per Main Idea. Write them down. Choose what you want to assess about them. *(Are they well connected to the theme? Do they sentences make sense?)* Give your partner a score! [Scoring: 1 is low and 5 is high.]

DRAW CONNECTIONS Look carefully at your Main Ideas. *Can you draw connections between the words?* Use blue (or black) lines to draw positive connections. Use red for negative connections. Don't worry! There are no "right" or "wrong" answers here. Do you best in making new and interesting connections. Have fun with this! This activity will really expand your mind and make you think about this topic deeper than before.

Section 4. Connection Analysis

Find six connections from Section 3. Write them in the white boxes. Think about your connections. *Why did you make these connections?* Write your reasons next to the white boxes. Be prepared to explain your reasons to your partner and your teacher.

Self-assessment: Choose what you want to assess. *How well did you do?* Give yourself a self-assessment (1 to 5).

Section 5. Partner's Connections!

Find a partner. Discuss the connections that your partner made. Write your partner's connections in the white boxes. Ask you partner why he/she made those connections. Write your partner's explanations in the space next to the white boxes.

Partner assessment: Choose what you want to assess. *How well did your partner do?* Give your partner a score (1 to 5).

Section 6. Paragraph Writing!

Choose two connections: Think about your connections. Draw two pictures about them. Write two short (3-4 sentence) paragraphs about them.

Partner's assessment: Exchange books with your partner. Choose how you want to assess your partner. *How well did your partner do?* Give your partner a score.

Teacher assessment: Show your work to your teacher. Receive assessment and paragraph writing advice.

Section 7. Better Paragraphs!

Make your paragraphs even better! Think about what your partner and teacher said. Write your connections in the white boxes. Draw new pictures. Write better paragraphs!

Was your partner helpful? Think about your partner's advice. How helpful was your partner? Give your partner a score (in your own book -you don't have to show your partner this score.)

Teacher's assessment. Receive a score from your teacher. Get advice too!

OPTIONAL: IMAGINATION EXPRESS

Look carefully at the picture. *What do you see?*

Adverbs: *Which adverbs match the picture? Write a few adverbs in the box.*

Adjectives: *Which adjectives match the picture? Write a few adjectives in the box.*

Use your adverbs and adjectives to make interesting sentences about the picture.

Deep Understanding Score: Read your sentences to yourself. Think about your sentences. Give yourself a *Deep Understanding Score*.

OPTIONAL: THINK AGAIN

Think about what you have accomplished during this unit. Answer the four questions. Take your time. (Write good, well-developed answers to the questions.) Use these answers to help your future studies.

SELF-ASSESSMENT SHEET (PRE)

NAME: DATE:

	LEVEL (1-5 stars)	COMMENT:
Reading	☆ ☆ ☆ ☆ ☆	_____
Writing	☆ ☆ ☆ ☆ ☆	_____
Listening	☆ ☆ ☆ ☆ ☆	_____
Speaking	☆ ☆ ☆ ☆ ☆	_____
Grammar	☆ ☆ ☆ ☆ ☆	_____
Vocabulary	☆ ☆ ☆ ☆ ☆	_____
Spelling	☆ ☆ ☆ ☆ ☆	_____
Presentations	☆ ☆ ☆ ☆ ☆	_____
Overall Fluency	☆ ☆ ☆ ☆ ☆	_____

Section 1. Introduction

Look at the picture above. Ask and answer "who, what, when, where, why, how" questions.

Your questions	Your answers	Partner's answers
Q1. What do you see?		
Q2. _____		
Q3. _____		
Q4. _____		

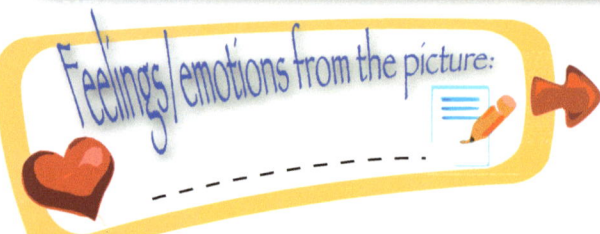

Performance of Understanding Time!

Discussion:
"This picture makes me feel…"

Section 2. Word map to expression!

 Choose your own Root Word from the picture in Section 1 and create a word map.

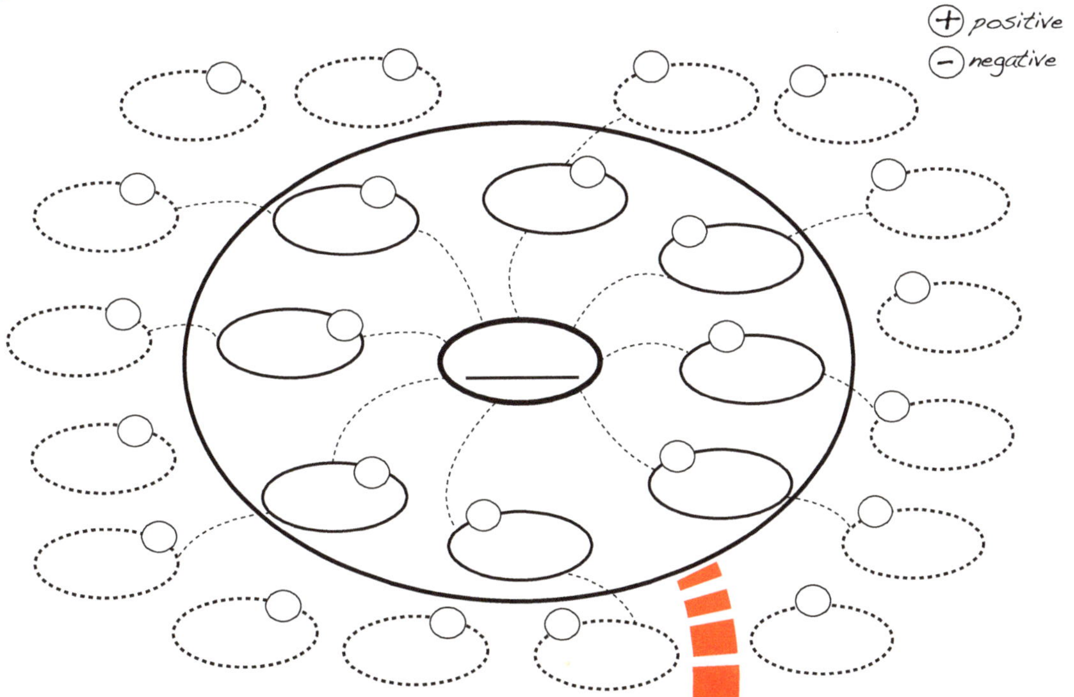

⊕ positive
⊖ negative

Find three main ideas from your word map! Write them in the boxes below.

Main Idea 1

Main Idea 2

Main Idea 3

Self-assessment of ideas: 1 2 3 4 5 (low – high)

Section 3. Expansion

Think about your three Main Ideas. Write them below. Also write down the Linguistic, Socio-cultural, and Feelings/Emotional connections you find.

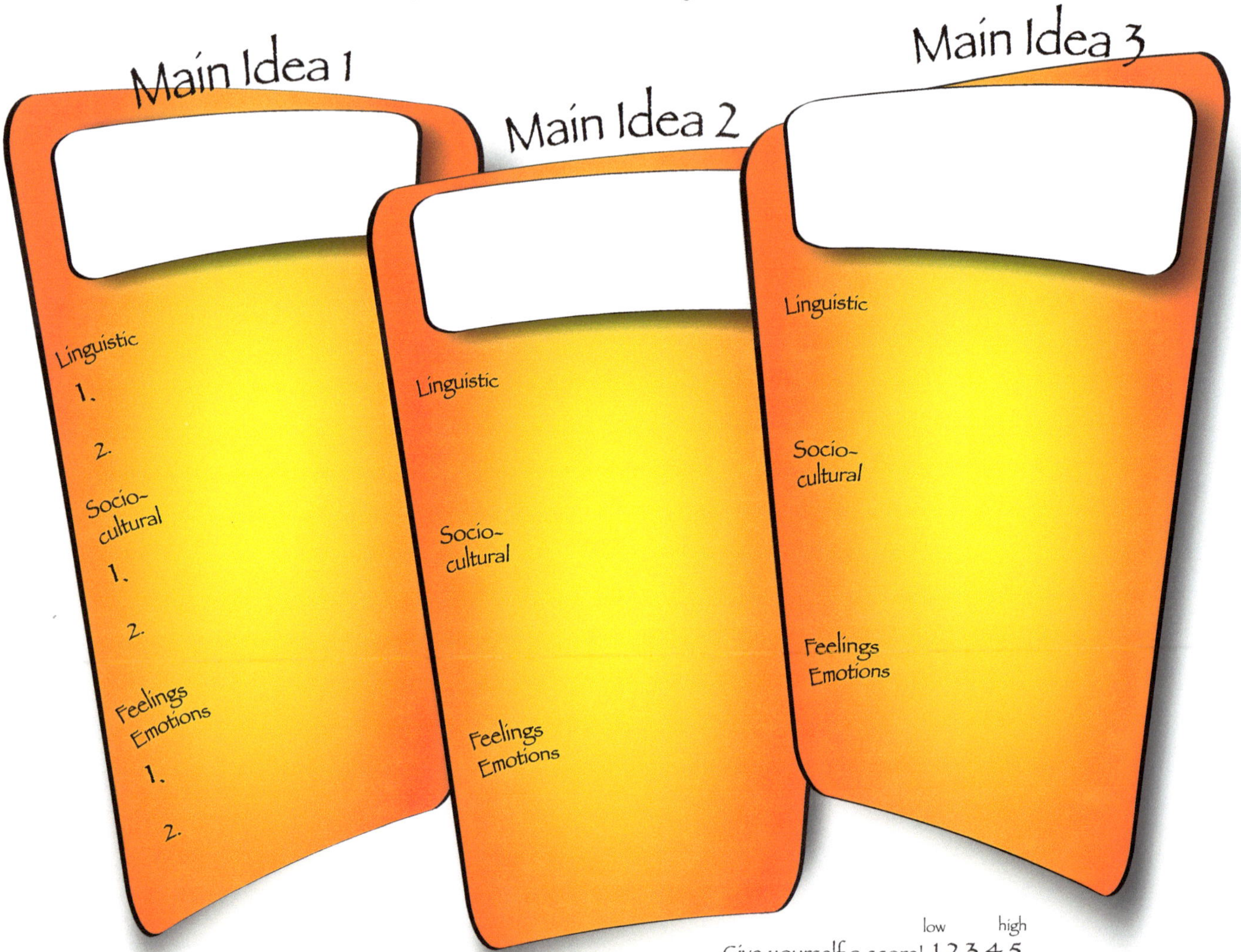

Main Idea 1

Linguistic
1.
2.

Socio-cultural
1.
2.

Feelings Emotions
1.
2.

Main Idea 2

Linguistic

Socio-cultural

Feelings Emotions

Main Idea 3

Linguistic

Socio-cultural

Feelings Emotions

Give yourself a score! 1 2 3 4 5
low   high

DRAW CONNECTIONS

Blue/black for positive connections!
Red for negative connections!

Section 4. Connection Analysis!

Find six connections from Section 3. Write them down in the boxes below. Explain the connections.

Explain the connection!

1. Connection!

2. Connection!

3. Connection!

4. Connection!

5. Connection!

6. Connection!

low high
Self-assessment: 1 2 3 4 5

Section 5. Partner's Connections!

Ask you partner about his/her connections. Write them down in the boxes below.

1. Connection! Explain the connection!
2. Connection!
3. Connection!
4. Connection!
5. Connection!
6. Connection!

Partner assessment: 1 2 3 4 5
                       low   high

Section 7. Better Paragraphs!

Make your paragraphs even better!

Connection!

Picture!

Connection!

Picture!

Was your partner helpful?
Score your partner's help level: [1 2 3 4 5]

low high
Teacher's assessment: 1 2 3 4 5

OPTIONAL

IMAGINATION EXPRESS

Look carefully at the picture above. Think of matching adverbs and adjectives.
Write them down. Make sentences.

Adverbs for this picture.

Adjectives for this picture.

Score: shallow 1 2 3 4 5 deep

OPTIONAL

THINK AGAIN

Think about the unit you just finished. Answer these questions.

1. What did you enjoy about this unit?

2. How can you connect what you learned to the real world?

3. What have you become interested in because of this unit?

4. Ideas for improving your skills:

low   high
Self-assessment: 1 2 3 4 5

Section 1. Introduction

Look at the picture above. Ask and answer "who, what, when, where, why, how" questions.

Your questions	Your answers	Partner's answers
Q1. What do you see?		
Q2. _____		
Q3. _____		
Q4. _____		

 Feelings/emotions from the picture:

 Performance of Understanding Time!

Discussion:
"This picture makes me feel…"

Section 2. Word map to expression!

 Choose your own Root Word from the picture in Section 1 and create a word map.

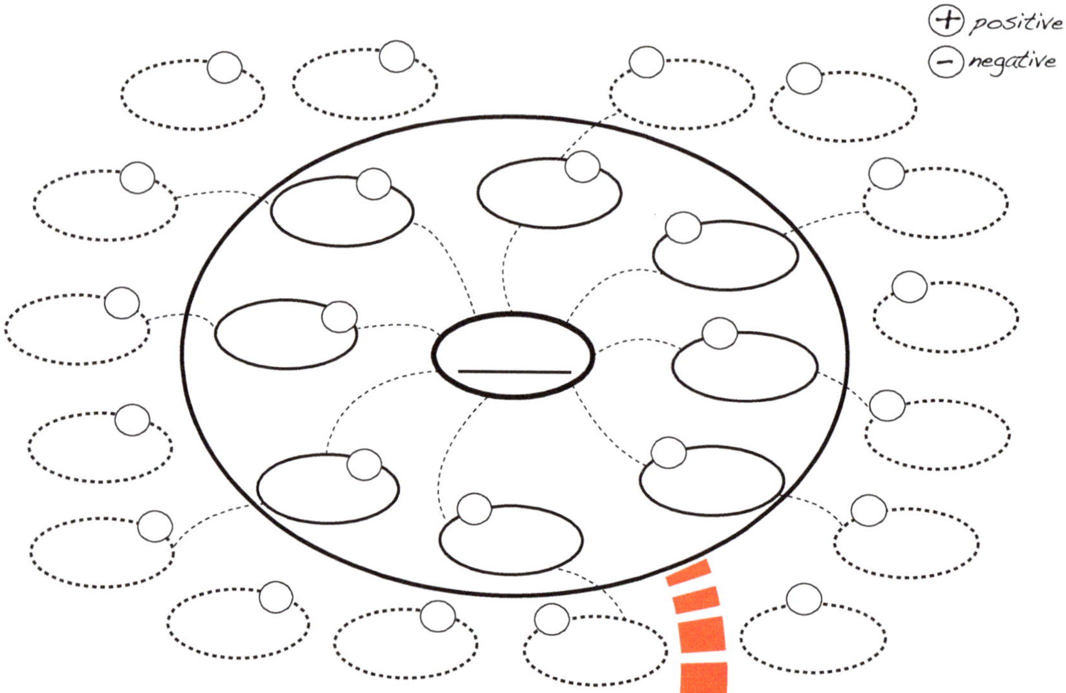

⊕ positive
⊖ negative

Find three main ideas from your word map!
Write them in the boxes below.

Main Idea 1

Main Idea 2

Main Idea 3

Self-assessment of ideas: 1 2 3 4 5 (low — high)

Section 3. Expansion

Think about your three Main Ideas. Write them below. Also write down the Linguistic, Socio-cultural, and Feelings/Emotional connections you find.

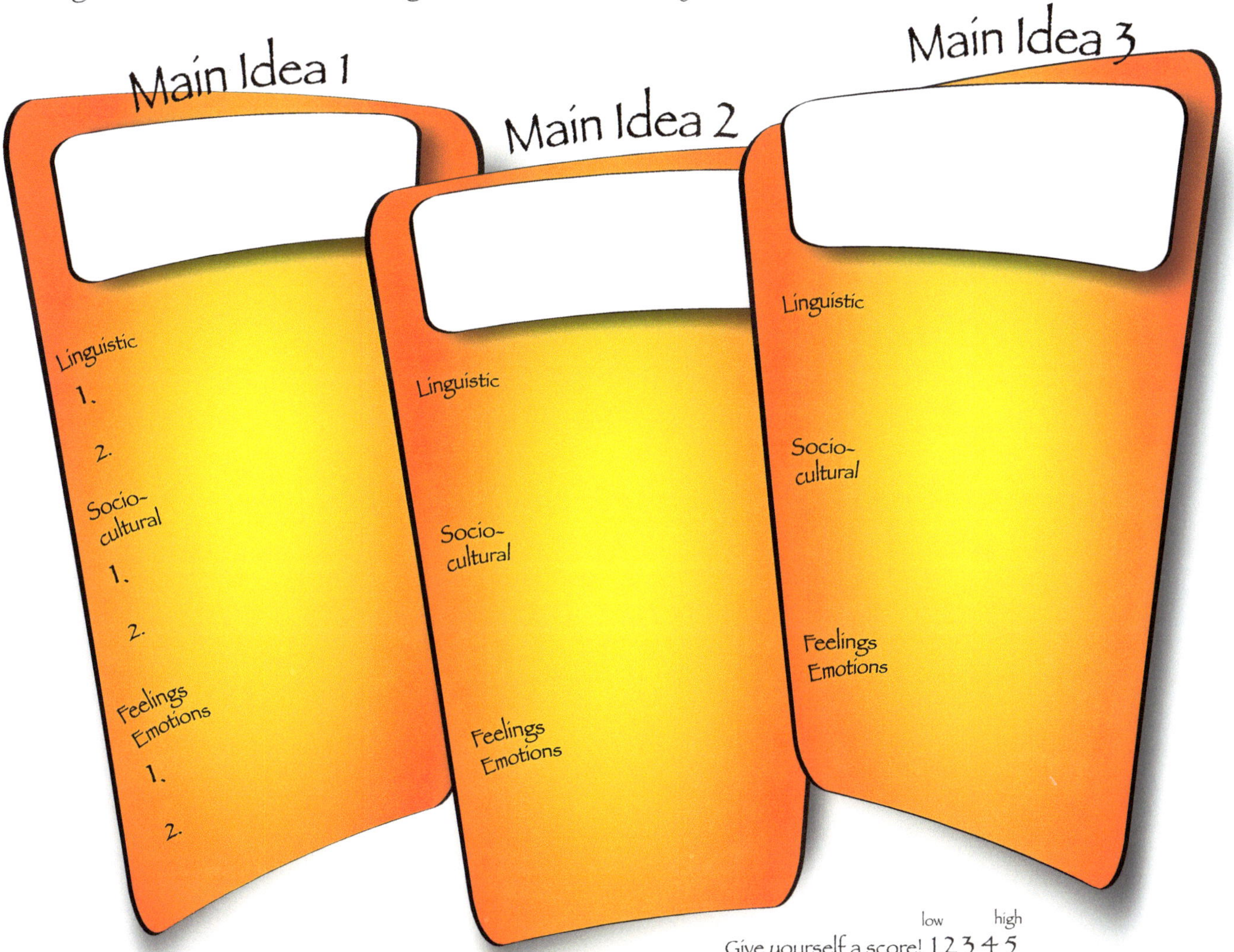

Main Idea 1

Linguistic
1.
2.

Socio-cultural
1.
2.

Feelings Emotions
1.
2.

Main Idea 2

Linguistic

Socio-cultural

Feelings Emotions

Main Idea 3

Linguistic

Socio-cultural

Feelings Emotions

Give yourself a score! low high
1 2 3 4 5

DRAW CONNECTIONS

Blue/black for positive connections!
Red for negative connections!

Section 4. Connection Analysis!

Find six connections from Section 3. Write them down in the boxes below. Explain the connections.

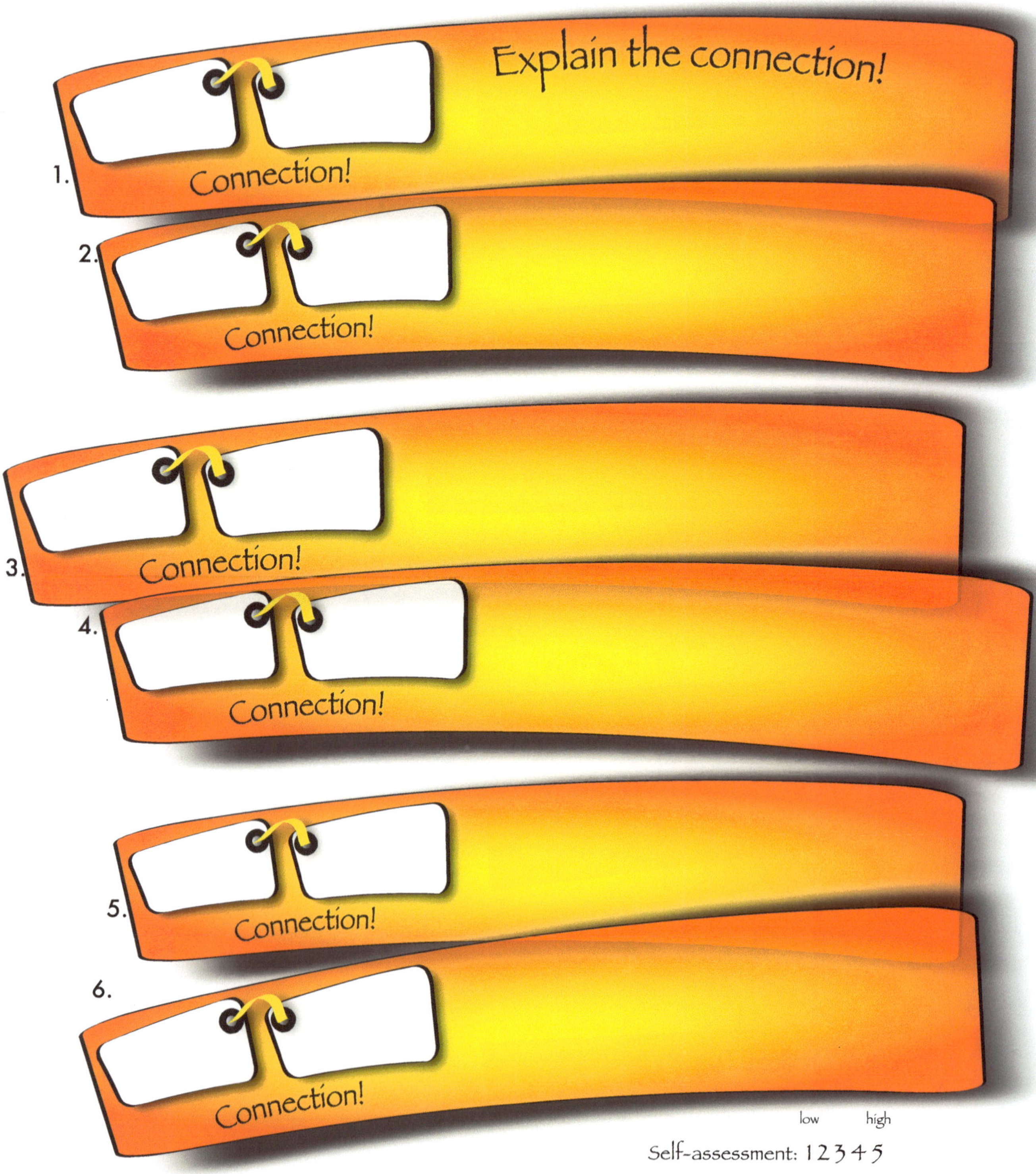

Explain the connection!

1. Connection!

2. Connection!

3. Connection!

4. Connection!

5. Connection!

6. Connection!

low   high
Self-assessment: 1 2 3 4 5

Section 5. Partner's Connections!

Ask you partner about his/her connections. Write them down in the boxes below.

Explain the connection!

1. Connection!
2. Connection!
3. Connection!
4. Connection!
5. Connection!
6. Connection!

Partner assessment: 1 2 3 4 5 (low – high)

Section 6. Paragraph Writing!

Write paragraphs using your connections! Draw pictures too! Get advice.

Picture!

Connection!

Picture!

Connection!

low   high
Partner's assessment: 1 2 3 4 5
Teacher's assessment: 1 2 3 4 5

Section 7. Better Paragraphs!

Make your paragraphs even better!

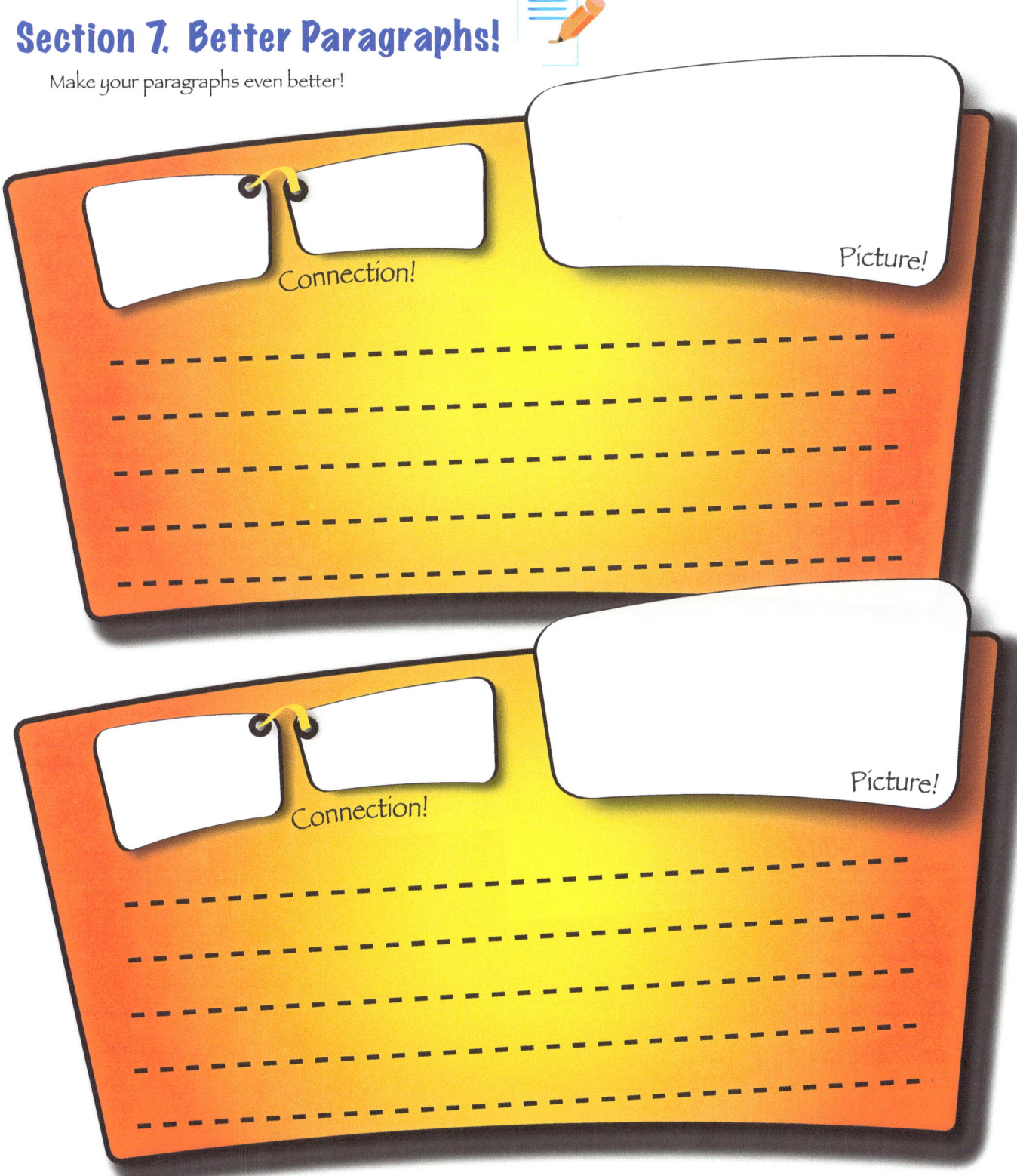

Was your partner helpful?
Score your partner's help level: [1 2 3 4 5]

low   high
Teacher's assessment: 1 2 3 4 5

OPTIONAL

IMAGINATION EXPRESS

Look carefully at the picture above. Think of matching adverbs and adjectives.
Write them down. Make sentences.

Adverbs for this picture.

Adjectives for this picture.

Score: shallow 1 2 3 4 5 deep

OPTIONAL

THINK AGAIN

Think about the unit you just finished. Answer these questions.

1. What did you enjoy about this unit?

2. How can you connect what you learned to the real world?

3. What have you become interested in because of this unit?

4. Ideas for improving your skills:

low　　high
Self-assessment: 1 2 3 4 5

Section 1. Introduction

Look at the picture above. Ask and answer "who, what, when, where, why, how" questions.

Your questions	Your answers	Partner's answers
Q1. What do you see?		
Q2. _____		
Q3. _____		
Q4. _____		

Feelings/emotions from the picture:
_ _ _ _ _ _ _ _

Performance of Understanding Time!

Discussion:
"This picture makes me feel…"

Section 2. Word map to expression!

 Choose your own Root Word from the picture in Section 1 and create a word map.

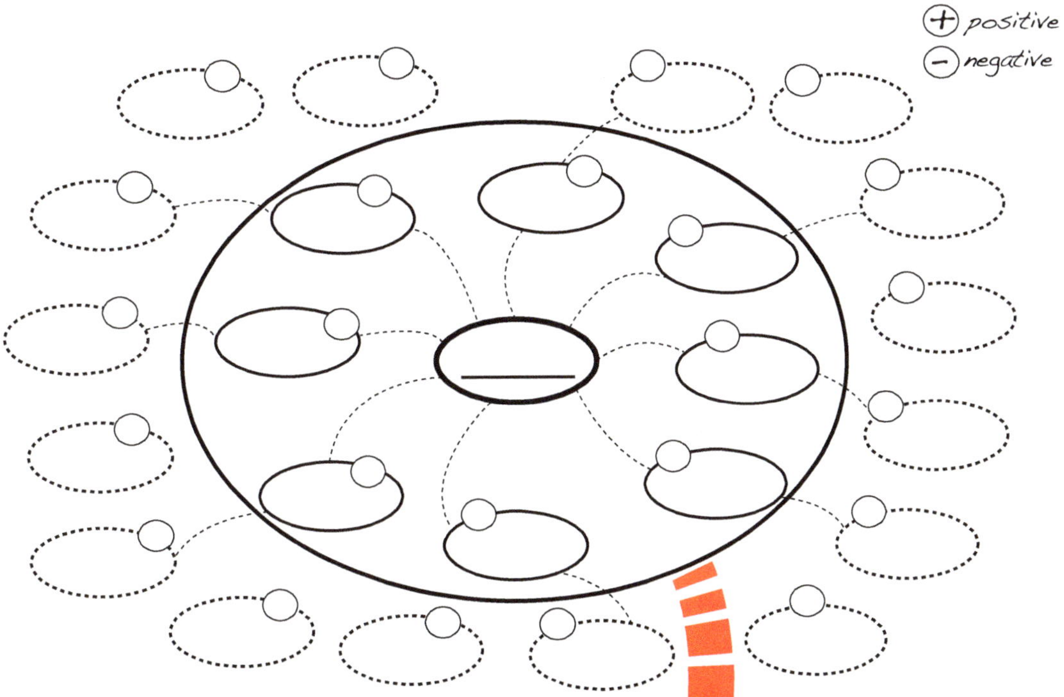

⊕ positive
⊖ negative

Find three main ideas from your word map!
Write them in the boxes below.

Main Idea 1

Main Idea 2

Main Idea 3

Self-assessment of ideas: 1 2 3 4 5
(low — high)

Section 3. Expansion

Think about your three Main Ideas. Write them below. Also write down the Linguistic, Socio-cultural, and Feelings/Emotional connections you find.

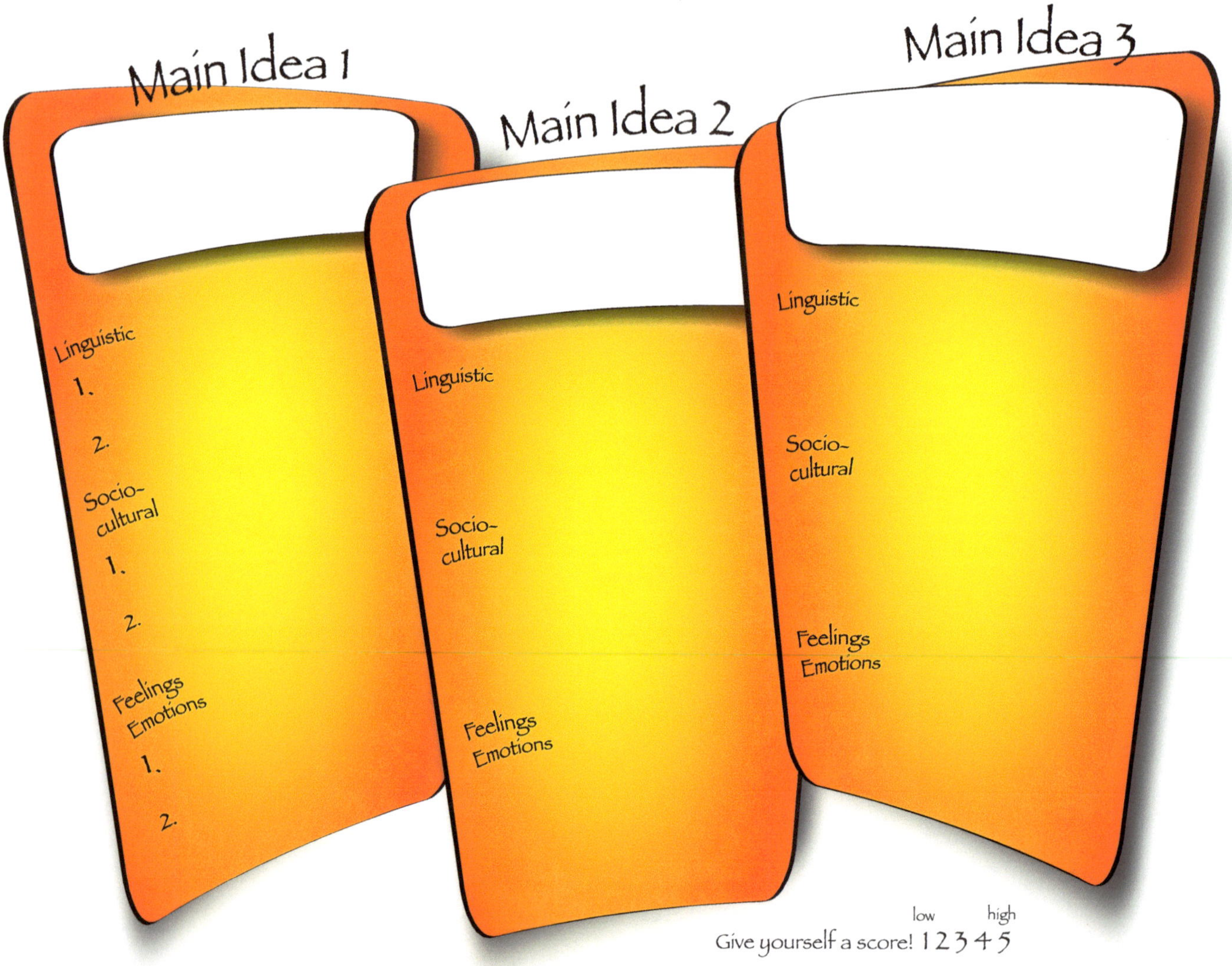

Main Idea 1

Linguistic
1.
2.

Socio-cultural
1.
2.

Feelings Emotions
1.
2.

Main Idea 2

Linguistic

Socio-cultural

Feelings Emotions

Main Idea 3

Linguistic

Socio-cultural

Feelings Emotions

Give yourself a score! low high
1 2 3 4 5

DRAW CONNECTIONS

Blue/black for positive connections!
Red for negative connections!

Section 4. Connection Analysis!

Find six connections from Section 3. Write them down in the boxes below. Explain the connections.

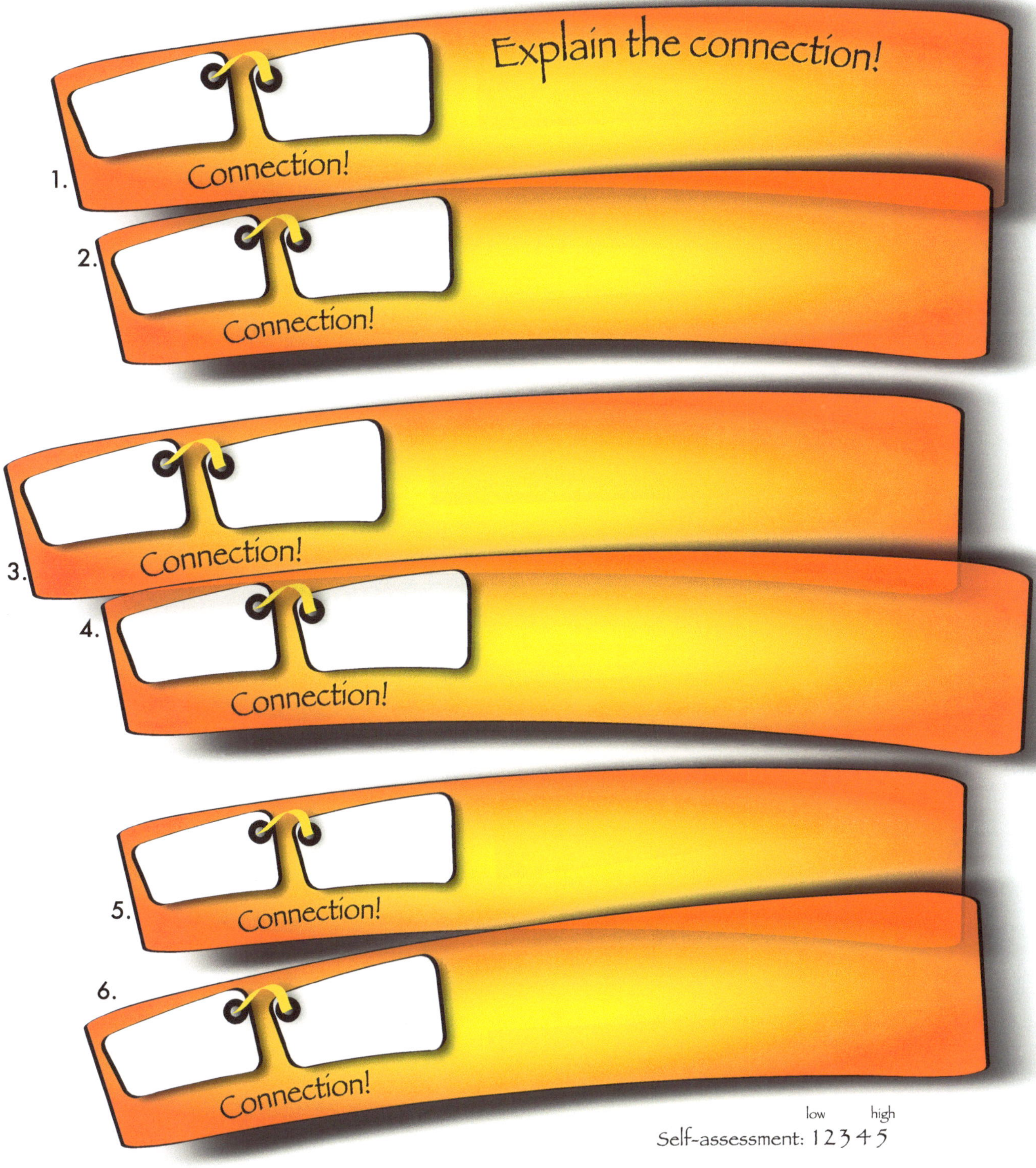

Explain the connection!

1. Connection!

2. Connection!

3. Connection!

4. Connection!

5. Connection!

6. Connection!

Self-assessment: 1 2 3 4 5
                          low   high

Section 5. Partner's Connections!

Ask you partner about his/her connections. Write them down in the boxes below.

Explain the connection!

1. Connection!

2. Connection!

3. Connection!

4. Connection!

5. Connection!

6. Connection!

Partner assessment: 1 2 3 4 5
(low — high)

Section 7. Better Paragraphs!

Make your paragraphs even better!

Was your partner helpful?
Score your partner's help level: [1 2 3 4 5]

low   high
Teacher's assessment: 1 2 3 4 5

OPTIONAL

IMAGINATION EXPRESS

Look carefully at the picture above. Think of matching adverbs and adjectives.
Write them down. Make sentences.

Adverbs for this picture.

Adjectives for this picture.

Score: shallow 1 2 3 4 5 deep

OPTIONAL

THINK AGAIN

Think about the unit you just finished. Answer these questions.

1. What did you enjoy about this unit?

2. How can you connect what you learned to the real world?

3. What have you become interested in because of this unit?

4. Ideas for improving your skills:

low　high
Self-assessment: 1 2 3 4 5

Module 4
Night Life

Section 1. Introduction

Look at the picture above. Ask and answer "who, what, when, where, why, how" questions.

Your questions	Your answers	Partner's answers
Q1. What do you see?		
Q2. ____		
Q3. ____		
Q4. ____		

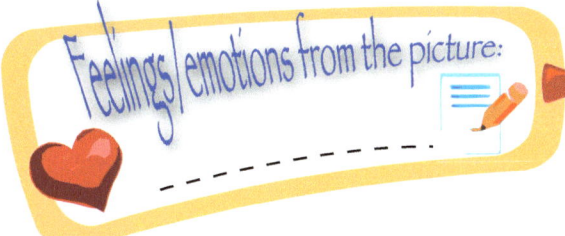

Feelings/emotions from the picture:
_ _ _ _ _ _ _ _ _ _

Performance of Understanding Time!

Discussion:
"This picture makes me feel…"

Section 2. Word map to expression!

 Choose your own Root Word from the picture in Section 1 and create a word map.

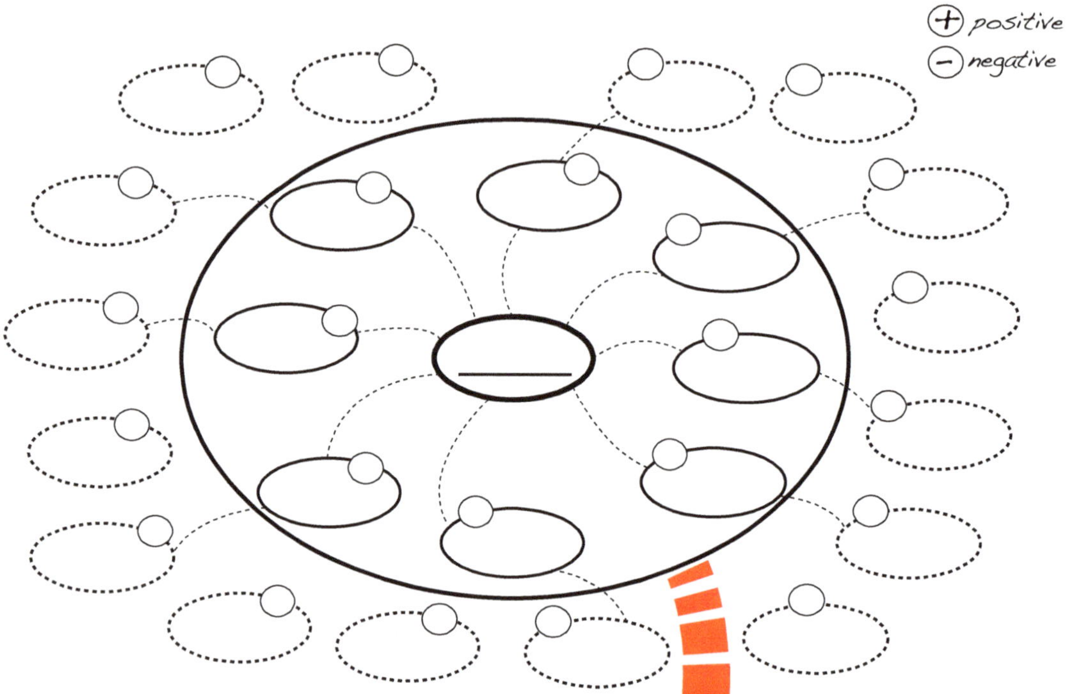

⊕ positive
⊖ negative

Find three main ideas from your word map!
Write them in the boxes below.

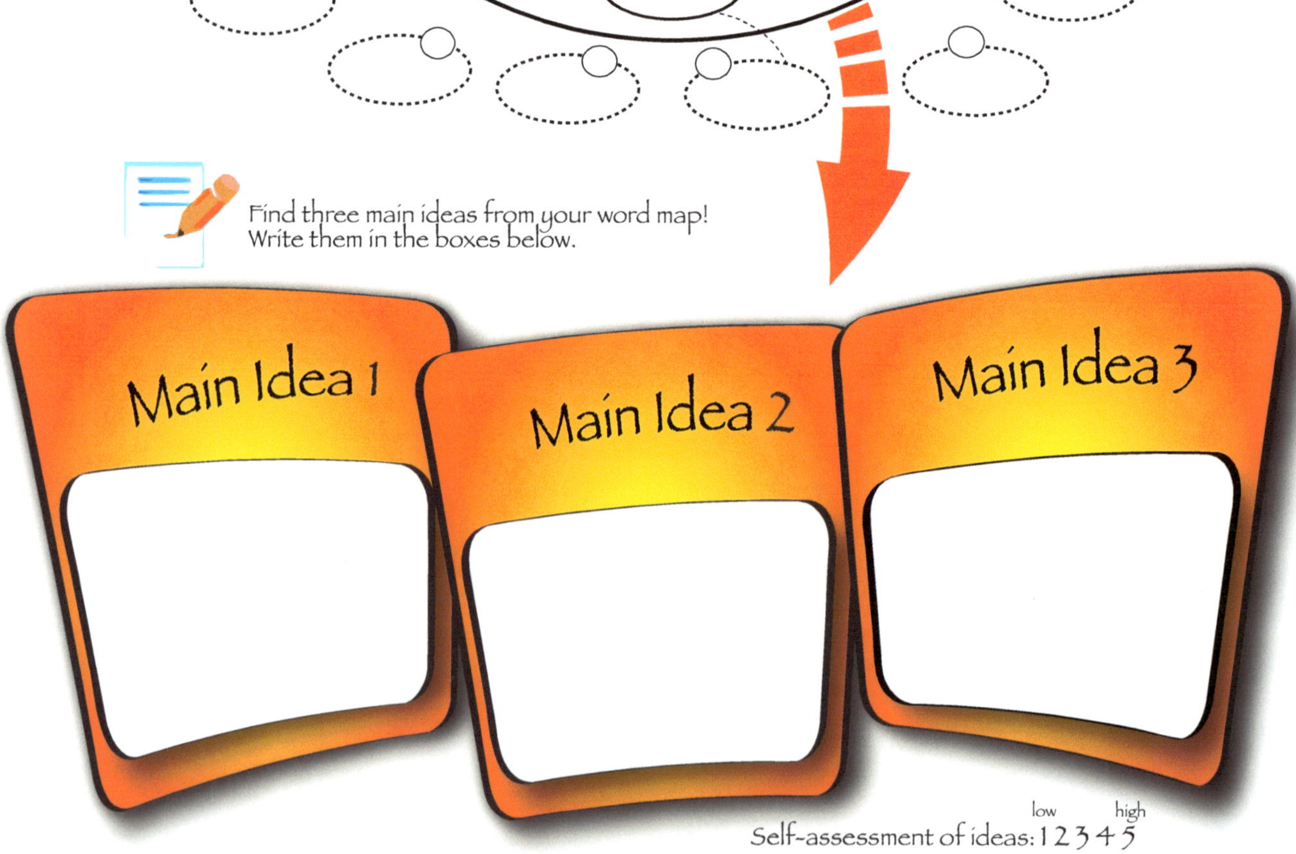

Main Idea 1

Main Idea 2

Main Idea 3

Self-assessment of ideas: 1 2 3 4 5
(low — high)

Section 3. Expansion

Think about your three Main Ideas. Write them below. Also write down the Linguistic, Socio-cultural, and Feelings/Emotional connections you find.

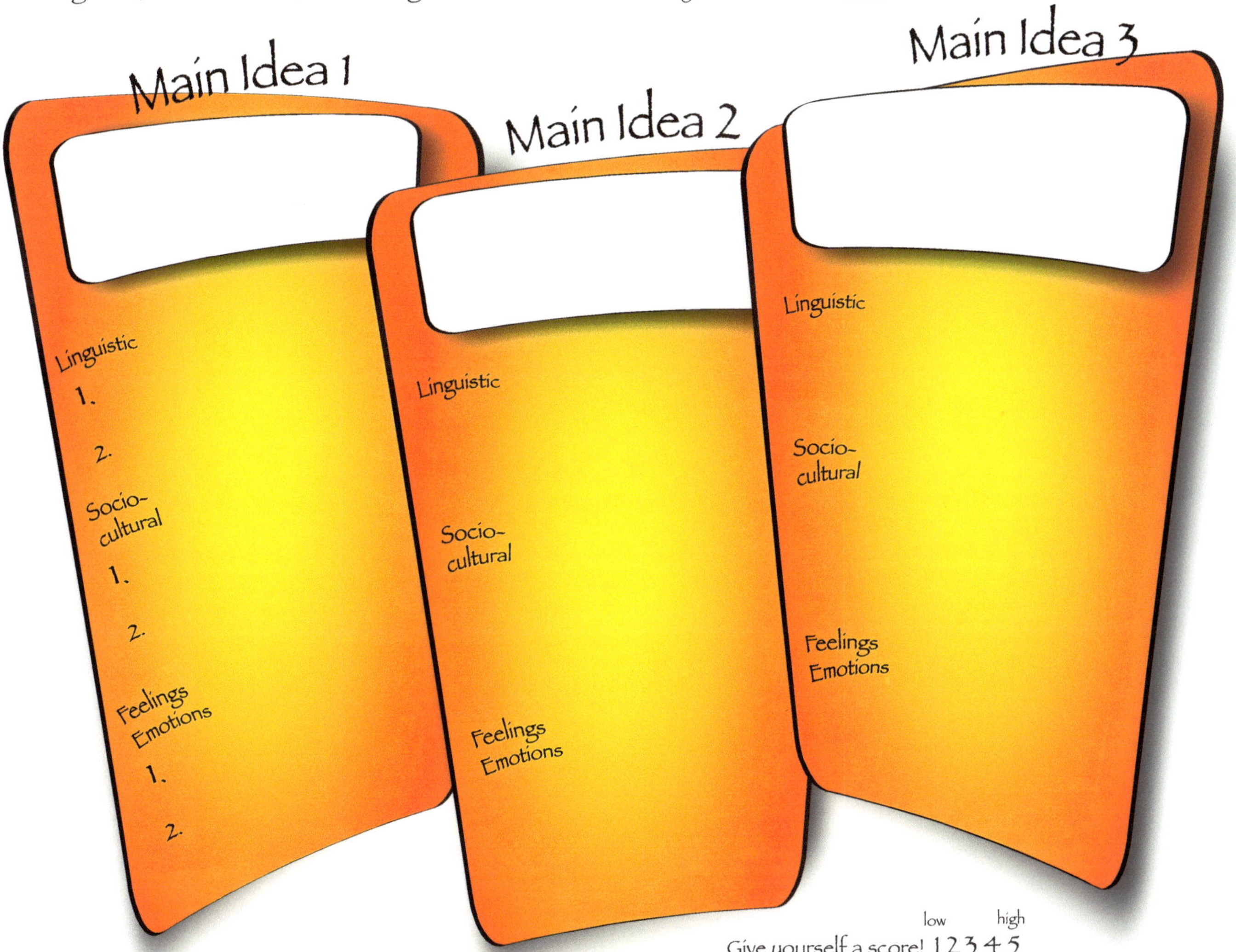

Main Idea 1

Linguistic
1.
2.

Socio-cultural
1.
2.

Feelings Emotions
1.
2.

Main Idea 2

Linguistic

Socio-cultural

Feelings Emotions

Main Idea 3

Linguistic

Socio-cultural

Feelings Emotions

low   high
Give yourself a score! 1 2 3 4 5

DRAW CONNECTIONS

Blue/black for positive connections!
Red for negative connections!

Section 4. Connection Analysis!

Find six connections from Section 3. Write them down in the boxes below. Explain the connections.

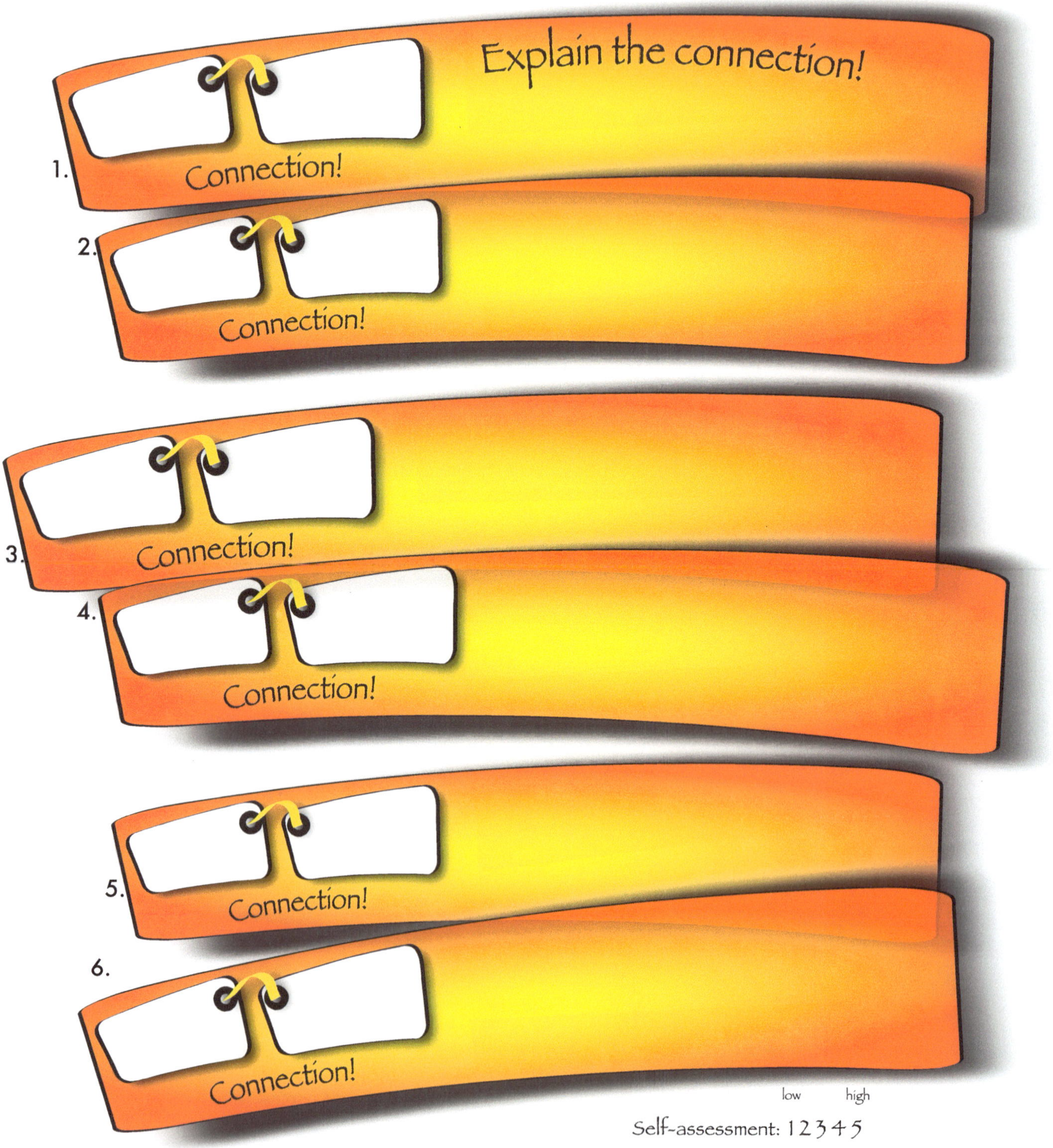

Explain the connection!

1. Connection!

2. Connection!

3. Connection!

4. Connection!

5. Connection!

6. Connection!

low   high
Self-assessment: 1 2 3 4 5

Section 5. Partner's Connections!

Ask you partner about his/her connections. Write them down in the boxes below.

Explain the connection!

1. Connection!

2. Connection!

3. Connection!

4. Connection!

5. Connection!

6. Connection!

Partner assessment: 1 2 3 4 5
(low — high)

Section 6. Paragraph Writing!

Write paragraphs using your connections! Draw pictures too! Get advice.

Picture!

Connection!

Picture!

Connection!

low   high
Partner's assessment: 1 2 3 4 5
Teacher's assessment: 1 2 3 4 5

Section 7. Better Paragraphs!

Make your paragraphs even better!

Was your partner helpful?
Score your partner's help level: [1 2 3 4 5]

low   high
Teacher's assessment: 1 2 3 4 5

OPTIONAL

IMAGINATION EXPRESS

Look carefully at the picture above. Think of matching adverbs and adjectives. Write them down. Make sentences.

Adverbs for this picture.

Adjectives for this picture.

shallow   deep
Score: 1 2 3 4 5

OPTIONAL

THINK AGAIN

Think about the unit you just finished. Answer these questions.

1. What did you enjoy about this unit?

2. How can you connect what you learned to the real world?

3. What have you become interested in because of this unit?

4. Ideas for improving your skills:

Self-assessment: 1 2 3 4 5
(low — high)

Section 1. Introduction

Look at the picture above. Ask and answer "who, what, when, where, why, how" questions.

Your questions	Your answers	Partner's answers
Q1. What do you see?		
Q2. _____		
Q3. _____		
Q4. _____		

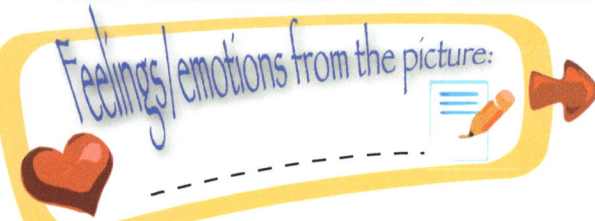
Feelings/emotions from the picture: _____

Performance of Understanding Time!

Discussion:
"This picture makes me feel…"

Section 2. Word map to expression!

 Choose your own Root Word from the picture in Section 1 and create a word map.

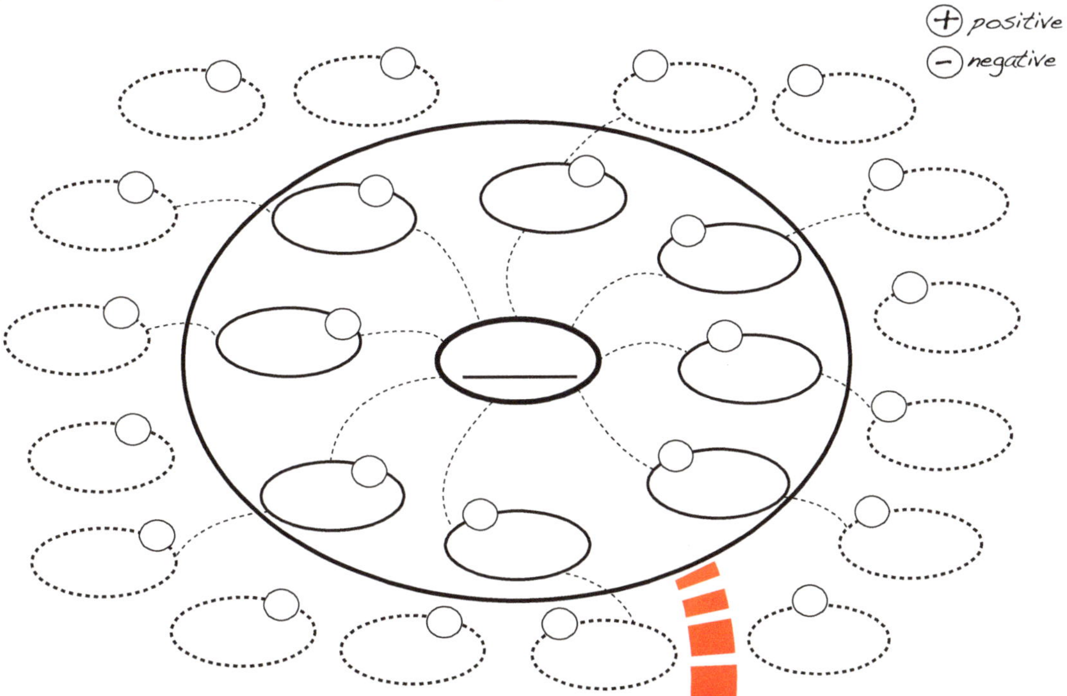

⊕ positive
⊖ negative

Find three main ideas from your word map!
Write them in the boxes below.

Main Idea 1

Main Idea 2

Main Idea 3

Self-assessment of ideas: 1 2 3 4 5
(low – high)

Section 3. Expansion

Think about your three Main Ideas. Write them below. Also write down the Linguistic, Socio-cultural, and Feelings/Emotional connections you find.

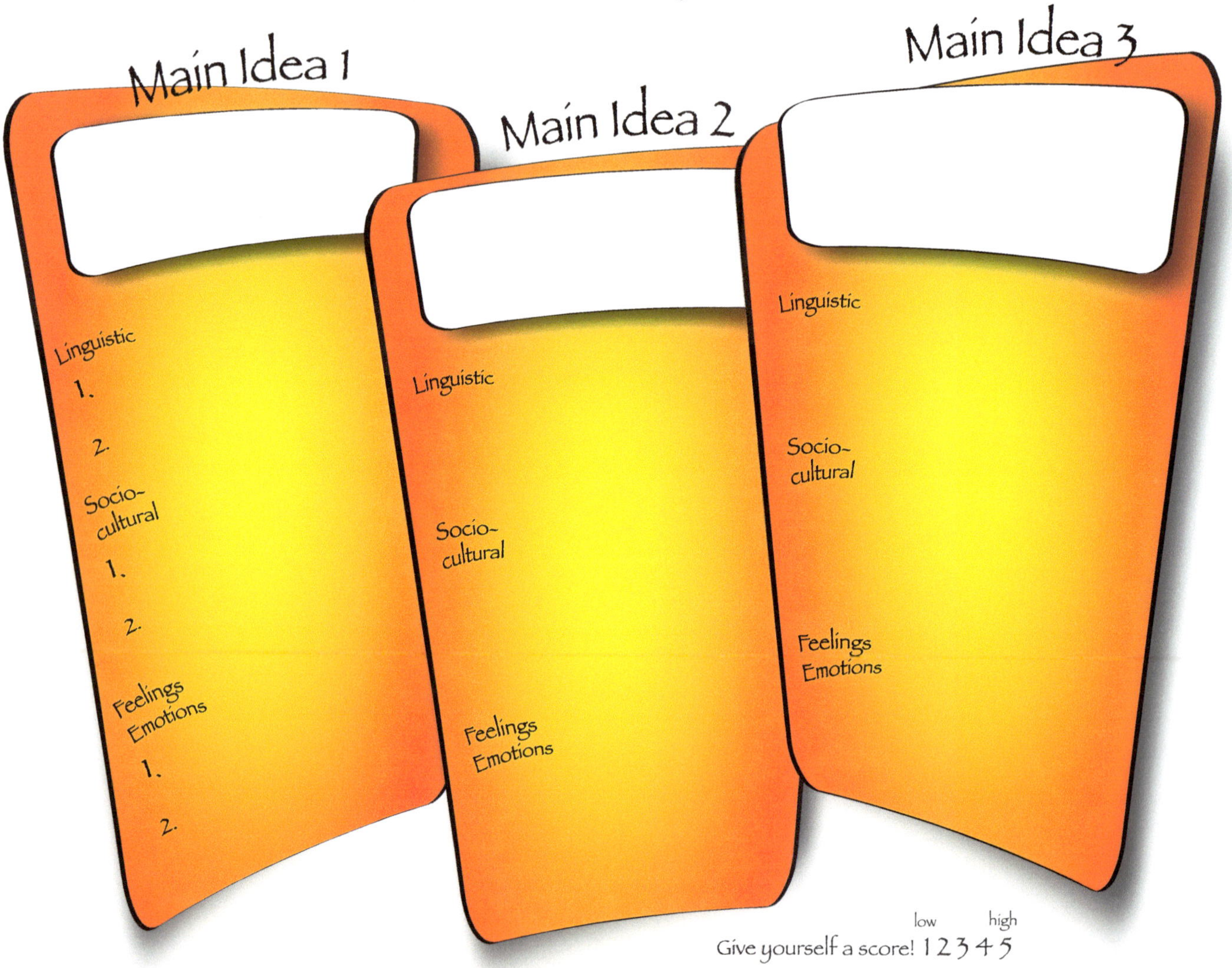

Main Idea 1

Linguistic
1.
2.

Socio-cultural
1.
2.

Feelings Emotions
1.
2.

Main Idea 2

Linguistic

Socio-cultural

Feelings Emotions

Main Idea 3

Linguistic

Socio-cultural

Feelings Emotions

Give yourself a score!   low   high
1 2 3 4 5

DRAW CONNECTIONS

Blue/black for positive connections!
Red for negative connections!

Section 4. Connection Analysis!

Find six connections from Section 3. Write them down in the boxes below. Explain the connections.

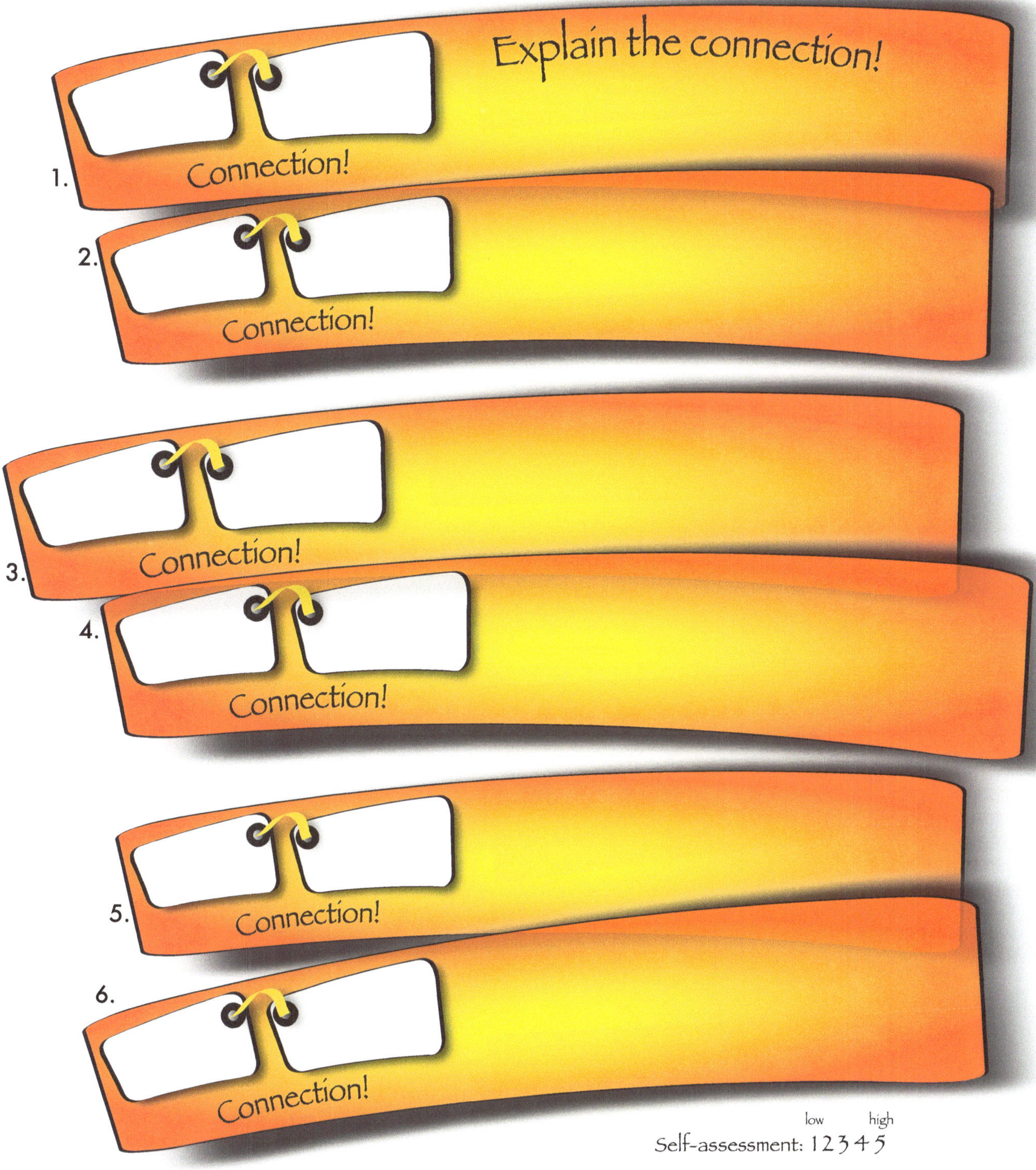

Explain the connection!

1. Connection!

2. Connection!

3. Connection!

4. Connection!

5. Connection!

6. Connection!

Self-assessment: 1 2 3 4 5 (low — high)

Section 5. Partner's Connections!

Ask you partner about his/her connections. Write them down in the boxes below.

1. Connection! Explain the connection!
2. Connection!
3. Connection!
4. Connection!
5. Connection!
6. Connection!

Partner assessment: 1 2 3 4 5 (low – high)

Section 6. Paragraph Writing!

Write paragraphs using your connections! Draw pictures too! Get advice.

Partner's assessment: 1 2 3 4 5
Teacher's assessment: 1 2 3 4 5

Section 7. Better Paragraphs!

Make your paragraphs even better!

Was your partner helpful?
Score your partner's help level: [1 2 3 4 5]

low high
Teacher's assessment: 1 2 3 4 5

OPTIONAL

IMAGINATION EXPRESS

Look carefully at the picture above. Think of matching adverbs and adjectives. Write them down. Make sentences.

Adverbs for this picture.

Adjectives for this picture.

shallow   deep
Score: 1 2 3 4 5

OPTIONAL

THINK AGAIN

Think about the unit you just finished. Answer these questions.

1. What did you enjoy about this unit?

2. How can you connect what you learned to the real world?

3. What have you become interested in because of this unit?

4. Ideas for improving your skills:

Self-assessment: 1 2 3 4 5
                   low   high

Section 1. Introduction

Look at the picture above. Ask and answer "who, what, when, where, why, how" questions.

Your questions	Your answers	Partner's answers
Q1. What do you see?		
Q2. ____		
Q3. ____		
Q4. ____		

Feelings/emotions from the picture:
_____

Performance of Understanding Time!

Discussion:
"This picture makes me feel…"

Section 2. Word map to expression!

 Choose your own Root Word from the picture in Section 1 and create a word map.

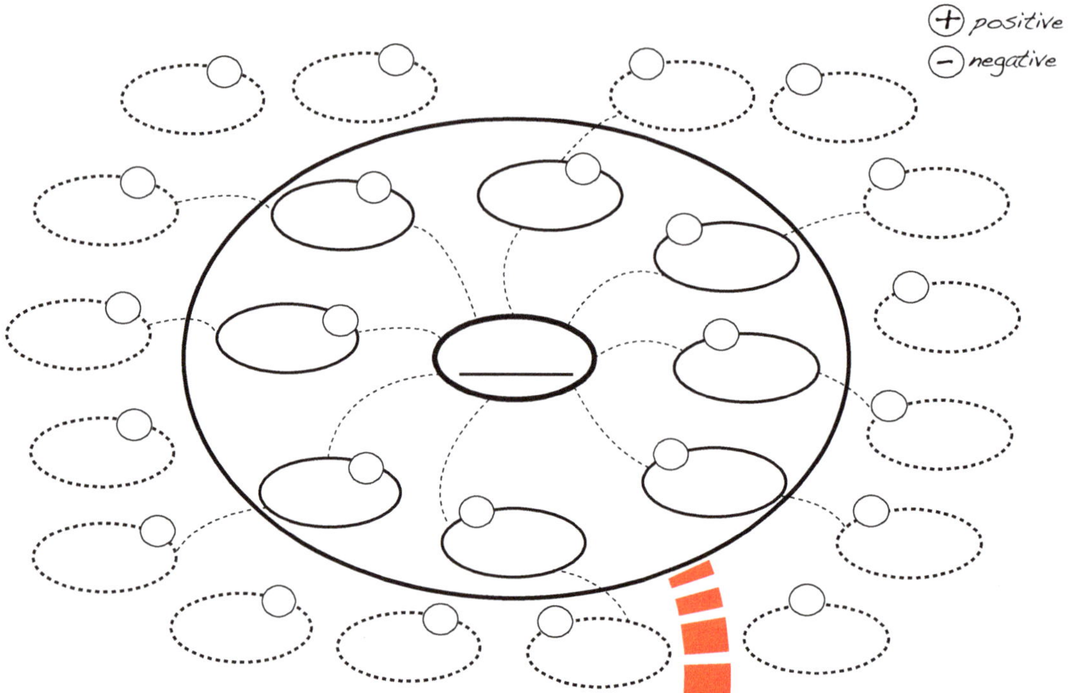

⊕ positive
⊖ negative

Find three main ideas from your word map!
Write them in the boxes below.

Main Idea 1

Main Idea 2

Main Idea 3

Self-assessment of ideas: 1 2 3 4 5 (low — high)

Section 3. Expansion

Think about your three Main Ideas. Write them below. Also write down the Linguistic, Socio-cultural, and Feelings/Emotional connections you find.

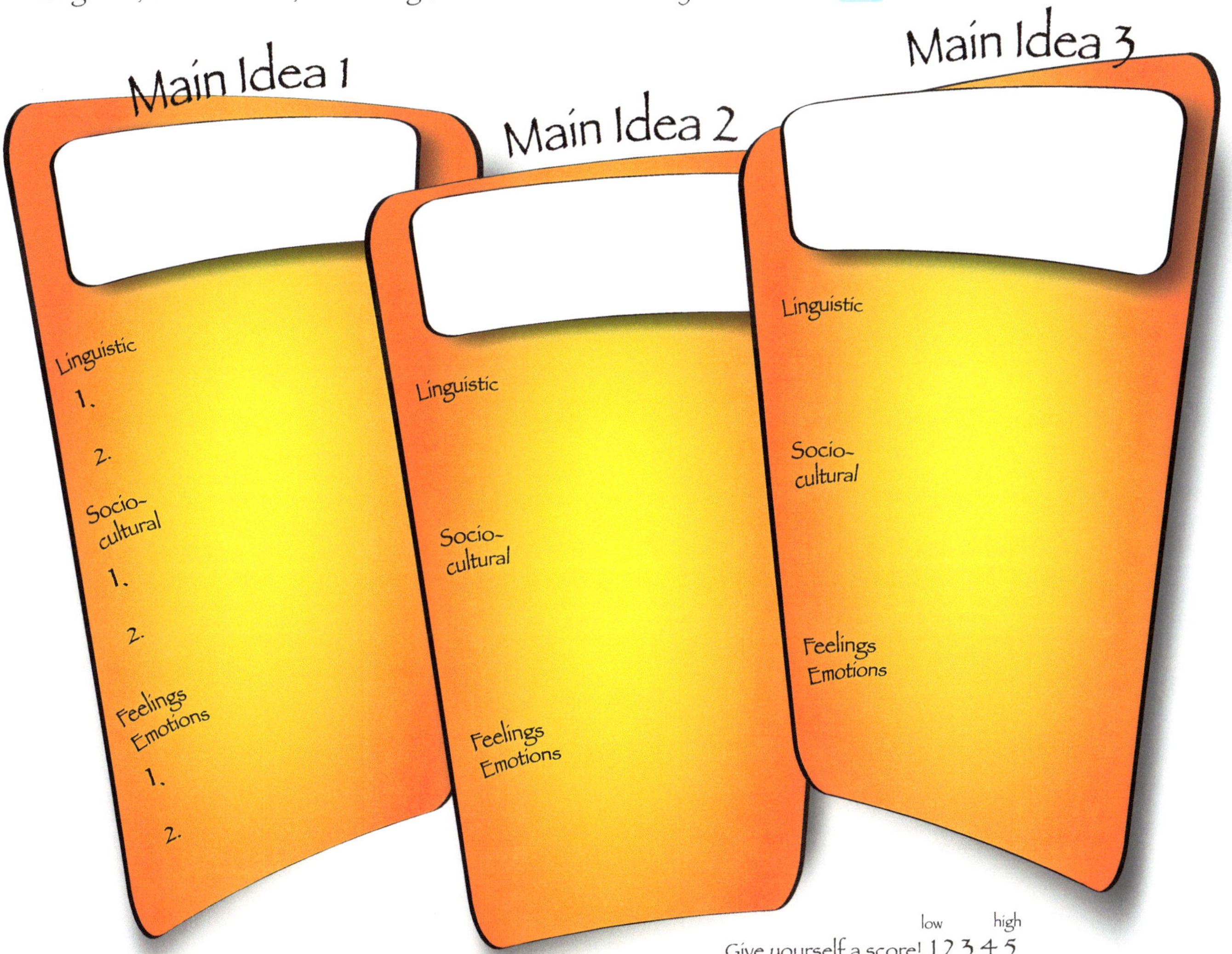

Main Idea 1

Linguistic
1.
2.

Socio-cultural
1.
2.

Feelings Emotions
1.
2.

Main Idea 2

Linguistic

Socio-cultural

Feelings Emotions

Main Idea 3

Linguistic

Socio-cultural

Feelings Emotions

Give yourself a score! 1 2 3 4 5
low   high

DRAW CONNECTIONS

Blue/black for positive connections!
Red for negative connections!

Section 4. Connection Analysis!

Find six connections from Section 3. Write them down in the boxes below. Explain the connections.

Explain the connection!

1. Connection!

2. Connection!

3. Connection!

4. Connection!

5. Connection!

6. Connection!

Self-assessment: 1 2 3 4 5
low — high

Section 5. Partner's Connections!

Ask you partner about his/her connections. Write them down in the boxes below.

Explain the connection!

1. Connection!
2. Connection!
3. Connection!
4. Connection!
5. Connection!
6. Connection!

Partner assessment: 1 2 3 4 5 (low — high)

Section 6. Paragraph Writing!

Write paragraphs using your connections! Draw pictures too! Get advice.

Partner's assessment: 1 2 3 4 5
Teacher's assessment: 1 2 3 4 5

Section 7. Better Paragraphs!

Make your paragraphs even better!

Connection!

Picture!

Connection!

Picture!

Was your partner helpful?
Score your partner's help level: [1 2 3 4 5]

low   high
Teacher's assessment: 1 2 3 4 5

OPTIONAL

IMAGINATION EXPRESS

Look carefully at the picture above. Think of matching adverbs and adjectives.
Write them down. Make sentences.

Adverbs for this picture.

Adjectives for this picture.

shallow   deep
Score: 1 2 3 4 5

OPTIONAL

THINK AGAIN

Think about the unit you just finished. Answer these questions.

1. What did you enjoy about this unit?

2. How can you connect what you learned to the real world?

3. What have you become interested in because of this unit?

4. Ideas for improving your skills:

low   high
Self-assessment: 1 2 3 4 5

NOTES

SOME HELPFUL ADVERBS!

carefully
correctly
eagerly
easily
fast
loudly
patiently
quickly
quietly
well

always
every
never
often
rarely
seldom
sometimes
usually

SOME HELPFUL ADJECTIVES!

angry
clumsy
defeated
embarrassed
fierce
grumpy
helpless
itchy
jealous
lazy
mysterious
nervous
obnoxious
panicky
repulsive
scary
thoughtless
uptight
worried

brave
calm
delightful
eager
faithful
gentle
happy
jolly
kind
lively
nice
obedient
proud
relieved
silly
thankful
victorious
witty

SOME MORE ADJECTIVES!

alive
careful
clever
dead
easy
famous
helpful
important
inexpensive
odd
powerful
rich
shy
tender
uninterested
vast
wrong

beautiful
clean
elegant
fancy
glamorous
handsome
long
magnificent
old-fashioned
plain
sparkling
ugliest

boiling
broken
bumpy
chilly
cold
cool
creepy
cuddly
curly
damaged
damp
dirty
dry
dusty
filthy
flaky
fluffy
hot
warm
wet

NOTES

SELF-ASSESSMENT SHEET (POST)

NAME: DATE:

                                    LEVEL (1-5 stars)   COMMENT:

Reading   ☆ ☆ ☆ ☆ ☆   _____

Writing   ☆ ☆ ☆ ☆ ☆   _____

Listening   ☆ ☆ ☆ ☆ ☆   _____

Speaking   ☆ ☆ ☆ ☆ ☆   _____

Grammar   ☆ ☆ ☆ ☆ ☆   _____

Vocabulary   ☆ ☆ ☆ ☆ ☆   _____

Spelling   ☆ ☆ ☆ ☆ ☆   _____

Presentations   ☆ ☆ ☆ ☆ ☆   _____

Overall Fluency   ☆ ☆ ☆ ☆ ☆   _____

TEXTBOOK ASSESSMENT

1. Did this textbook (Optimal Levels!) help improve your English?   YES / NO

2. Comment:

3. What did you like about this textbook?

4. Which 'flavor' are you most interested in for your next textbook? (circle)

      Fun Flavor   Medical Flavor   Business Flavor

      Festival Flavor   Philosophical Flavor   Original Flavor

      Other _____   WHY? _____

www.ingramcontent.com/pod-product-compliance
Lightning Source LLC
Chambersburg PA
CBHW041526220426
43670CB00002B/43